The Sand that Burns.
The Rain that Bites.

Hannah Afzal

BookLeaf Publishing

Presentation by *BookLeaf Publishing*

Web: www.bookleafpub.com

E-mail: info@bookleafpub.com

ISBN: 9789357212717

First edition 2023

Dedicated to everyone who has had a role in my life - you've influenced me in some way that has shaped me into the person I am today. Thank you.

Dedicated to the orphans around the world. I pray one day you find warm arms that keep you safe and happy.

ACKNOWLEDGEMENT

I would like to express my sincere gratitude to my mother and father. As every single beat of my heart is powered by the endless love you both gave to me throughout my life.

Write Without Rules! Only Then Will You Be Free

مام Maam

I wish to write
Not words that are black and white
But words that contain, that create every colour

The blue from the tears that pool in their eyes
The white in the clothes that make up their souls
The red in the blood that seeps from their hearts
The black in the spine that carries the world

I wish to write words that are poetry

My love for it, I believe, stems from you
The way a branch stems from a tree
The way a thorn stems from a rose

It will be my way
of talking, of singing, of shouting
My way to be heard
For I feel I have been crushed into silence

But I fear
The words that I urge to write

have now the same fate
as the oppressed words trapped in my head
whenever I wish to speak

My fingers tremble with weight
of expectation, of judgement, of retribution
How do I set them free?
How do I stain my paper with ink?

Hannah

You are me as I am you
I am you as I was your grandfather
Through the passing of time
With every speck of sand flown into the past
With every drop of water rooting into the future
What he passed onto me, I have passed onto you

You have the ability to write
It is a power you hold within yourself
Within your blood
Within your heritage

Your soul is made up of those colours
Of the blues, the whites, the reds, the black
Your soul is made up of the sand
that has flown through millennia
Your soul is made up of the rain

that have nurtured infinite

Let it fall from your fingers as ink
The way pain falls from your eyes as tears

مام Maam

If only you knew, I think to myself
If only she knew that her poetry was magic
That her fingers were delicate flowers
That her ink was the galaxy

The same poetry I see in one's tears
The same poetry I see in a burning candle
The same poetry I see in the day-lit moon
The same poetry I see in submission to my Lord

I wish she knew that her words
created the definition
of grace, of beauty
Infinite, endless
And that my pen and ink
would only limit.

Hannah

Just write.

Forget the rules
Forget the people
Forget the world.

And write

The words within you are ready to be set free
Without expectation, without judgement,
without retribution
Just write
And I promise you

You will write poetry
Your words will be poetry

The Only Thing I Have Is My Name

The only thing I have is my name

Before my birth
Before my mother's blood filled my veins
Before time grew me a heavy heart, a silent
tongue, an empty mind

Even before I was a body of light
fulfilled, satiated and glowing
Just as I imagine the angels would be
in the darkest, sun-stricken of rooms

The only thing I had then was my name
Then only thing I have now is my name
My only identity
My only pillar of strength

Where are you from, they ask?
Panick
Well...I was born in Scotland

As I stand under the cold rain, I feel it
Each drop travelling all the way from the
heavens

It bites into me
Penetrates past every layer of cloth
Branding into my skin, occupying the territory
in my veins
It entwines with my blood
As bold as a lover reuniting with the beloved
after millennia apart

I feel cold and yet I cling to the familiarity of it
The rain is mines
It belongs to me just as I belong to it
It is a victim of my identity just as I am a victim
of it's sharp presence
It covered me at birth
It covers me now

Well, I was born in Scotland
And lived here my entire life
Is that not enough?

Hesitate
Well...where are you from...
Originally?

One small word
and my presence, my being, my identity
turns into dust that falls behind
and will never be able to keep up

Oh. Well my parents were born in Pakistan.
They are Pakistani
I am Pakistani

If I say it out-loud, will that make it true?
If my ink stains it on paper, will that declare it?
If I whisper it in my prayers will He will it into
existence?

Will it mark into my future and preserve itself in
history?

I am Pakistani. I am Pakistani. I am Pakistani
I shout and I shout and I shout
And yet they only laugh

You are not
I am not
You cannot speak the language
I cannot
You do not know of your ancestors, your people,
your land, your caste
I do not
You are not knowing of it's struggle!

You are not Pakistani

The sand burns beneath my feet
the hot sun sinks it's rays into each speck of
earth
and turns the earth golden
so golden, like the colour of my skin
so golden, that it burns

And all of the unborn sadness
that occupies my eyes, my brain, my body
a merciless cancer
falls from my body like rainwater and sinks into
the sand

Now
The sand looks like my eyes
And my body is an easy hollow
a warm glow
Is this what home feels like?

My cousins run past me
Run! Run fast!
We need to reach the cart!
Otherwise he will leave us behind

The sand fills my legs and feet with power
And I run
Hot, its sting powered by courage I envy
But slippery, and I stumble with every stride

My cousins grab my left arm
My sisters grab my right
and they pull me up to them onto the cart
Breathless but pride swelling my heart
I look around and I see

I see
my people
my village
my country
my home

I see the strong buffalo dragging the cart
I see the beehive of villagers selling and
conversing
I see people on motorcycles and families on
rickshaws
I see the sun standing tall claiming its space
I see my home

They say I am not Pakistani, but how can I not
be?
When anytime I look into the mirror
I see a reflection of Pakistan itself

Golden skin, the colour of burnt sand
Brown eyes rich as the fertile soil the west
would rage war over

Hooked nose shaped by my grandfather and
generations before him
Black, thick hair like the coat of the buffalo
carrying my cousins

I am Pakistani, I think to myself as the rain bites
at me
I am but I am not
I am Scottish but I am not

Despite the beauty I see in the grey skies and
regardless of the fact
when I speak, rugged "R's" and silent "T's" are
what comes out
No matter how many hills I climb or how many
crops I grow
No matter how many Scottish songs I sing and
dances I dance
No matter how many years I spend serving the
people of this country
No matter how hard I push myself to thrive and
grow in this endless, cold rain
They will never fully accept me and I will never
be Scottish.

Because when they see, they see someone born
from the sand.
And when the others look at me, they see
someone born from the rain.

And I find myself asking

If I ground myself in the Scottish soil, will I
become a part of it?
If I bury my body in the Pakistani sand, will I
become a part of it?

For the rest of my life, will I just be a luminal
space?

A throughway from one area to the other
That feeling of altered reality, of eeriness, of
void space
A limbo
A path
Neither an arrival or a destination

Empty car parks, airport corridors, bedrooms at
3am, service stops, stairwells, train stations
Is my existence forever to be a luminal space
because I belong neither here or there
I will always be in the middle
Torn between two countries, two people, two
identities

This sense of loss is a book
And I have concluded that I don't have an
identity

Regardless of how badly I long for one
I only have my name

Born as Fatima
Lived as Hannah

It is as if my parents foreshadowed what would
become of me as soon as I was born

I only have my name
But I wonder if one day
The burning sun and the freezing rain
Will love me enough
To grow the roots I left behind
In the Scottish soil and the Pakistani sands
And I wonder if one day, they will eventually
meet and entwine

To form me an identity

So that I could live as a person
And not as an existence

Dad

You left me

To return to Him

For there is no greater place

But you took my happiness with you

And left me behind

Inner Child

I see you
Daydreaming, even as a child

You sit there and dream
Your imagination running wild
I can see it from the universe contained in your
eyes
The white, twinkling stars in the black, velvet
night

You sit, idle, but I know in your mind
you are bringing things to life
Creating characters, stories, adventures

I want to sit by you
but I worry I might frighten you
Let me stay here then, so I may protect you from
a distance

I see a plethora of dark brown curls
hand-painted from God himself
I see cheeks full of youth, round like the moon
Heavy, they force a downward frown

I see the gentle rise and fall of your shoulders
Steadiness that becomes a form of meditation for
me

And finally I go back to your eyes
They continue to shine, so innocent, so pure
As if your eyes had not glimpsed anything since
Heaven itself

My throat tightens, my heart clenches
Tears form and fill my eyes
But seeing the girl in front of me
This feeling is not enough for my tears to break
through

This is not sadness nor is it happiness
Seeing her fills me with deep love
Yet she also breaks me into pieces

What happened to you, I think?
How did it end up like this?

Why has my face sunken in, cheekbones as
sharp as knives
Why has my body folded in on itself, as if I am a
fleeting paper plane
Why, with every inhalation of air, I feel as if I
cannot breathe?

The colour of your presence no longer gleams as
my mothers refuge
It is now another shade made opaque by the
world's paintbrush
I realise that as time continues to pass, my
colour will start to wash out
And I will only continue to fade

O my sweet child, how the world has hurt you!

This is not sadness nor is this happiness
Is this grief?
No, not grief. Because she has not died
But I feel as if I am mourning her

For she is my past self
everything I was
and can never be again

She continues to daydream
so oblivious - it makes me want to laugh in
disbelief!
You make me so happy, yet so sad
So intense, this feeling
that has no name
that is between two homes

I cannot contain this within my chest
and so it creates tears that fall with a whisper
from my eyes
and I awaken you from your dream

I'm sorry

I sit next to you
And you are not scared
Because you know who I am
And even though I am you and you are me
You still look at me and think

What happened to her stars?

I tell you, do not worry
About anything
Let me sit with you
My inner child
And let us just be.

The Next Life

And who knows

Maybe in another life

We would have been

Lovers

Muse

I wonder if

After our eyes meet

for a fleeting second

I linger in your mind

The way you do in mines

When we pass one another

And our clothes brush against each other

We both know a connection is born

But do you feel as tied to me

As I do to you?

And when you speak

Your voice, it caresses my ears

and becomes my poetry

But, tell me, will I ever become your muse?

My Death

What did it feel like? They say

It's strange.
Because, in a sense, it felt like I had been the
one to die
His soul had been the one to leave
But the only empty vessel was me

And was I ever truly alive?

Three days he was in a coma
Three days I was in limbo

That first night he died
I had died myself

And every day since
His body has disappeared but his soul is vibrant
My body is breathing but my heart is
asphyxiated

I felt like a ghost that first month
So empty
and transparent
Existing but not really alive

And nobody ever realised
when they spoke to me
I was never actually there

And why would they care?
They only had to say words
And then they carried on
Just like the world carries on
And leaves you in the dust

But there are no words
That can fix you
No gestures, no actions

My three siblings
Who each carry a quarter of my heart
No words leave their mouths
Because they are as I am
And feel how I feel

And how could they ever show it?
When they themselves are mirrors to my father

The eldest with her boldness
The second with her diligence
The youngest with his solitude
Me, with my spirit

To say it
Would be to declare it
To sever that connection we keep of him

We are pieces to a wider puzzle
And just like I died
I think so too did they
In a way

With every tear that dropped she said
That doesn't look like my dad
That isn't him
I can't recognise him

I guess from that moment
He finished his role as my father
And left the ending behind

And she was right
How could it have been him?
My dad was so big and so strong and so loud
and so tall
And so, so alive
But the body on the table was so still.

I refuse it to be him
And I will forever refuse it

Dad,

How could you have left me?
You were never mines, I know that
You always belonged to Him, I accept that
But how could you have left so early
When my life had barely even begun?

I never got the chance to thank you
For all your hard work
For all your hardships, your sacrifices and
efforts
For all your tears and emotions
That had been forced to be buried within you

I never had a chance
To give you
What the cruelty of this world
Robbed from you

Dad,

Did you not know
That you were my backbone?
Mum is my sword
But you were my shield
And now that you've gone
My defence is ruined
And my armour is in pieces

And how can I ever live again?
When my protector is gone
And I am left exposed to the world

You returned in the same land you were born in
You returned in the same month you were born
in
And yet you were not Home

Because the people lowering you into the ground
And the people that prayed your funeral prayers
Although they looked like you
They were strangers to me

Your home is here with us

But now that you've left
I guess it was only natural
That we too, were displaced

Dad,

I hope you know this
As a measure of my love for you
When you died
I felt as if I had, too.

-

May we reunite in Jannah through Allah SWTs
mercy

Guardian Angel(s)

Did you think I did not know?

That you two are the reason I fly

The world pushed me over the edge

When I was not ready

But you both wrapped your arms around me

And held me tight.

Because you two are of his blood

You will never admit

that it pains you to see my tears

Because in their reflection

you see your own sadness.

Pain that never healed

It turned into grief and buried itself deep within
you

Dormant, but never forgotten

And because of your love for me

you both ripped out a wing each

and rooted them into me

One on my left side and one on my right

And what are the oceans without the moon?

What is honey, without its mighty bee?

What is an angel without her wings?

You chose to sacrifice flight

So that I could soar the skies

You two became wingless

So that I could fly.

I see the blood that runs down your back

I see the pain, even when masked with smiles

You both became my Guardian Angels

Despite having not received any of your own

I do not think I will ever be able to repay

The love, the happiness, the warmth

The protection that I did not deserve.

But I want you to know that

With the wings you two gave me

I hope that one day

My feathers will stem your bleeding

And if the world ever pushes you over

I'll fly fast enough, to catch you both

And we can sail the skies

together

The Last of Her Kind

When the last petal falls from the flower she is

Will she realise she is the last of her kind?

Her silhouette, when she is praying

Will be the image forever imprinted in my mind

A Letter to The Moon

To, The Moon

My Queen

I see you

Standing tall and shining bright

You light up the black sea

With every night

Celestial beauty

The stars twinkle

with your kindness and with excitement

Because they say

You are not from this world.

Otherworldly

And you know it

Selene,

Your smile

So serene

Mischievous

Because you know

You can never be captured

Or contained

You are free

In all your glory and might

Tell me

How do I become like you?

Radiant and glowing

Royalty in the night

Yet your presence

Remains humble and quiet

Luna,

You make me feel safe

When I cannot sleep

All I have to do is look up to you

To see that you have already found me

And you give me a knowing smile

And a strong hug

As if we are old friends

From another lifetime

My Dear Moon

I guess I just wanted to say

Thank you

For being my quiet companion

My poetry's muse

My shining light

When the world is asleep

And I am alone at night

Love,

Hannah

Will You Stay...And Have a Cup of Chai With Me?

Chai is not a mere cup of tea
It is a potion, that can only be made by the
purest of magicians and the rustiest of cauldrons
It is an emblem of Pakistan itself; the concoction
brewed and perfected since the beginning of the
sands.

Chai is not a mere cup of tea
For people bound together by blood
It is at times a peace offering but mostly a
declaration
For love was something that was never verbal
And are we not people from a hard country?
The blacksmith sun hammered and shaped us
Our innate pride forming into armoured
exteriors
So we do not say "I love you", we say
"Sit and have some chai."

Chai is not a mere cup of tea
How can it be?
When my mother's heavenly hands pinch a
handful of fennel and cardamom
Only the universe is aware of the exact amounts

And I finally understand why I can never
replicate her chai
How can I?
When her poet hands travel me back eighteen
years
Wrapped in a musty cumble, relaxed and at ease.
The sweet fragrance that steams out my cup
turns into ink
That she uses to write into the thread of time
Her love for her children

So, I hope you know
That chai is not a mere cup of tea
It is an offering of my love for you
So, if I ask you to have a cup of chai
I am telling you I find you worthy of my love
And if you accept and drink
You are telling me, I love you too

And I see you lingering by the door
We have stopped talking
But we don't find this silence uncomfortable
In fact, it is an ease that only soulmates can ever
claim
But out of modesty, you take this as a signal to
leave
And for all the Sabr I have accumulated over
time
I cannot stand it, to see you go

And pull that golden thread that links us, further
apart
For the further you walk away
The thread wrapped around my heart threatens
to break it in half

So please

Will you stay...
And have a cup of chai with me?

Gym shoes

"I have spare shoes in my locker. You can use
them if you want?"

                                             "..."

"...Really?"

"Yeah, do you want me to get them?"

-

Strange
People have said words to me my entire life
But why were yours different?

Sunlight crept in
It did not flood or illuminate
It crept in
Quietly but reassuringly
As if it were a visitor
A friend

Bright enough for me to see the split in the rock
Warm enough for me to thaw out

A guide
A helping hand
To pull me out the dark, endless room
I had been submerged in

A lifeline

Did you know your words saved my life?

And do not misunderstand
People had said words my entire life
But theirs, like everything else in life, were
fleeting

And are we not mere strangers to one another?
Not even people
But till this day,
I ask
Why were your words different?

I guess I could find out
But I'm tired, I'm sorry
I think for once
The way you said those words without thinking
I wanted to receive without thinking

All I know was your words were warm and safe
When I had been cold for so long
So, I held on

And I kept them for myself

You lifted me up with that lifeline
Did you know?

You just said words but
Your words saved my life

Iffat

Virtue, do not worry

The world cannot see you the way I do

They cannot see your beauty

Cannot understand it

How could they?

Do they not know

That you are written

by an entirely different language?

A language born deep within the sands

That has brewed for years and birthed endless
generations

A language inked from the blackest of nights

Chastity, do not be sad

The language of your beauty

Expresses what they cannot even begin to
comprehend!

Your grace brings to life words that did not even
exist

And can you not see me

My muse

Using your rich, moon-like beauty

as ink

to write my poems?

The Cat Bus

How I have wished

To be stolen into the night

To be whisked away into a magical world

And find adventure

Filled with victory and blight

It doesn't exist though, I say,

waiting for the bus

Life is to always be plain and boring

And mundane and grey.

"Hurry and get on!" A voice says

"You're letting the cold in, can't you see?

Hurry, girl, I'm a busy person

Got things to do and places to be."

I look up to see the bus driver

And my face falls in disbelief and shock

"Oh my god, hen, come in

Don't just stand there and gawk!"

I pay for my ticket to Shawlands

And cannot help my disbelieving stare

The driver is a woman with a black pointy hat

Long robes and silver, magical hair.

She puffs from a long, wand-like pipe

And drives like a mad woman, so fast and crazy

The smoke dances and fills the air

Turning into magic and making me hazy

I blink and suddenly everything changes

I look around and I nearly curse

Holding tightly onto my seat, I scream

"Driver! How the heck am I on the cat bus?!"

"Weren't you listening to the story?

My adopted stray cat - I couldn't leave the poor
thing at home!

So, I put a spell on him and now he helps me fly
this thing

Goodness girl, don't you moan!"

We soar the Southside

The witch bus-driver and I

The cat smiles away with every pounce

Throwing us up fast and high

We fly alongside the clouds

Her magical stories making me laugh

I look down to see a tiny shawlands

And she says "Oh, is that your gaff?"

The Cat bus lands and crouches to let me off

I thank her for all the fun and bid her goodbye

"Adventure is always around you, girl, all you need to do

Is imagine it in your minds-eye.

So don't be hopeless and don't be blue.

You just need to believe in it, and it will come true"

Ayyub A.S.

Looking in the mirror

I see the reflection of a girl who is not whole

Words appear around me

Broken. Empty. Faulty. Sick

Is my existence to be defined by disease?

Will I never be complete again

Now that this illness has trapped me?

Will others never accept me

Now that I am not pure like them?

But then I remember

His story, his patience, his faith.

He told me

Chronic Illness is nothing to be ashamed of

I cry and then I nod and then I realise

Was Ayyub (A.S) not chosen by God Himself?

Self Made Woman

You are strong! You are powerful! She shouts

I cry and I cry and I nod
For I know I am
But only because she was
And am I not of her blood?
Do I not come from her lineage? This

Self-Made Woman

That is what you are
I remember it then
I remember it now

Clear as day in those old photographs
Clear as day in my vivid memories

Those challenging eyes
That expressive mouth
Legs that carried that tough body
From the pain of youth
And the struggle of old age

With a cigarette in your mouth
You put the men in their place

With your shouts and strong language
No fear at all
Only courage
And your boldness
I think it scared people
Certainly frightened me at times
But now I admire it

Your gentleness
It birthed an entire empire
And from your strength
We find inspiration to carry on
Your sweetness
It encouraged the turnip to grow
And helped soften my heart
God, how I miss it

Did you know
The crops don't grow anymore
Your legacy will never be forgotten
But still I tried to nourish the soil
To show that I, or the land, will never forget you
But they refuse to grow

All I wanted was to grow some turnips
So that I can be with you again
So that we can uproot and wash them
Lounge in our shalwaar kameez
And eat them raw in the garden

The sincerity of our efforts making them sweeter

But I suspect
When you passed
The land itself refused to be tamed
And of course, that was only natural
Why would they listen to my hands?

When they deserve the respect of the hands of

A Self-Made Woman

-

May Allah SWT reunite us in Jannah

"He is with you wherever you are." - Quran 57:4

When the world turns its back on me yet again

And when my own shadow disappears in the dark

I remember You

I pray You may forgive me

For how could I forget?

Are you not closer to me than my own jugular vein?

I work in health care

At the end of my shift

I leave the ward

Nightfall has landed and comfortable silence
welcomes my ears

I am so tired and so drained

Not physically or mentally

But something else entirely

I see this same feeling contained in the eyes

Of all the nurses and the doctors

And all the other staff I have the honour to work
alongside

What a pleasure it is to provide care to fellow
people in dire need of it

But how heart-breaking it is to see people at the
lowest point of their lives

Aren't we all soldiers fighting for the same cause?

These people lose pieces of themselves whilst fighting

But everyday we replenish them with bits of our own.

I Wish You Could See
Yourself From My Eyes

I can see us both in the scene of a film

In a cafe so quaint and homely

You sit and you talk and talk and talk

I watch and I listen and I nod and I hum

My hands wrap around a cup of hot chocolate

The perfect hand warmer - it makes me forget
the Scottish rain

Whereas your coffee stays untouched and grows
colder with time

Because you cannot stop your train of thought

You have so much to tell me and there is not
much time

Before life and adulthood force us to separate
again.

You talk about politics and science, experiences and research

You talk about religion and love, family and development

You speak words and, of course, they form poems around my head

And because I know you better than I know myself

You're thinking; I'm boring her or I'm blabbing or I don't even know what I'm saying

And in this relationship, I'll proudly say you're right most of the time

But in this case, I'm sorry, but you have never been more wrong

My dearest friend

I wish you could see yourself from my eyes

Because what you think of as self-insecurity

I see as poetry

Do you think I cannot see the entire galaxy
contained in your eyes?

Your mind contains the Milkyway

Your heart contains the stars

And your smile has the power to make Pluto feel
loved again

You know that words do not come easy to me

So, I fear I will never be able to tell you

That your character - your existence - is my own
personal sun

It warms me up from the inside

And shields me from the cold rain.

Did I ever tell you, that one day a person told me

Hannah, you are a flower waiting to bloom!

I wish I could hold you and shake you by the
shoulders

But not to tell you the exact same thing

For you are a flower

But you are not waiting to bloom

You have bloomed

But you have grown so, so tall

That you have reached the Heavens themselves

I hope one day

You believe in everything you are

And find the flower within yourself

The same flower I found

From the moment I saw you

His Tears

I have seen many people cry

But for some reason

His tears are the only ones that break me

For each tear is a reminder

That I have failed him

Am I not your guardian angel?

Is my only job not to protect you?

For someone so experienced in solitude

You'd think I'd recognise when Loneliness was
sitting beside you.

And of course he would have been your closest
friend growing up

Your heritage forced him upon you

The sands that birthed you wrapped him around
your neck

The world that took everything from you, only
left him behind.

I'm sorry

That I did not do more when I could have

I grew weaker over time

And I'm afraid you suffered as a result

Your tears

Did you know they break my heart?

For it meant the world had hurt you

You, who was so innocent and undeserving

Your heart, so pure, that I know the angels in
Heaven cradled it themselves

And God Himself, blessed us with your
existence

But you had a heart filled with love for Him

And in those early days, you could have so easily returned.

You hardly cry now

And although it pains me

I want to tell you

That it's okay to let your tears escape when your heart fills up with sadness

Don't be scared for there is no shame in tears

or expectation or judgement

And did not the manliest of men cry without shame?

I see you now

Taller than a mountain and as loud as a lion

You are like the sword of Ali (A.S)

Heroic and courageous

And people say you are like Dad

And whilst you do resemble him externally

Internally, I think you have the softness of Mum

And was it not her father who poured his soul
into you

And turned your skin from blue to golden?

I want you to know

That I wish upon you constant happiness and
companionship

And although your tears make me cry

Remember, there is no shame in crying or being
sad

Burning Roses

میم

میں آپ کے لیے ایک نظم لکھنا چاہتا تھا۔

اور سالوں سے میں نے الفاظ تلاش کرنے کی کوشش کی
ہے۔

لیکن میں نے محسوس کیا ہے کہ یہ واقعی ناممکن ہوسکتا
ہے۔

آپ کے لیے بہت خوبصورت شاعری ہے۔

جو سیاہی میں نہیں سما سکتا

آپ کو بیان کرنے کے لیے جو الفاظ درکار ہیں وہ موجود
نہیں ہیں۔

اور جو الفاظ زندہ رہتے ہیں وہ صرف آپ کو محدود کر
دیتے ہیں۔

پرندوں کی طرح آپ آزاد کرنا چاہتے ہیں۔

مجھے امید ہے کہ ایک دن آپ بھی اڑ جائیں گے۔

اور اس پنجرے سے بچیں جس میں دنیا نے آپ کو ڈالا ہے۔

آزادی سب سے کم ہے جس کے آپ حقدار ہیں۔

اور مجھے یہ پوچھنے پر افسوس ہے۔

لیکن ابھی کے لیے

کیا آپ میرے ساتھ رہ سکتے ہیں؟

اور مجھے پیار دیتے رہیں

صرف آپ ہی دے سکتے ہیں؟

-

Maam

I wanted to write a poem for you

And for years I have tried to find the words

But I have realised this might actually be
impossible

For you are beautiful fleeting poetry

That cannot be contained in ink

For the words needed to describe you simply do
not exist

And the words that live would only limit what
you are

Like the birds you wish to free

I hope one day you too can fly away

And escape the cage the world put you in

Freedom is the least of what you deserve

And I'm sorry to ask this

But for now

Can you please stay with me

And continue to give me a love

Only you can give?

www.ingramcontent.com/pod-product-compliance
Lightning Source LLC
LaVergne TN
LVHW021229200726
843509LV00012B/1462